Journey's End

Relics and ruins of Indiana's transportation legacy

Passenger Depot (Lake Shore & Michigan Southern
Railroad, 1900)—Elkhart, Elkhart Co. (851.02)

Photography by John Bower

Text by John Bower and Lynn Bower
Foreword by Brian Byrn

 STUDIO INDIANA®

Published by:

STUDIO INDIANA®

430 N. Sewell Road   Bloomington, IN 47408

(812) 332-5073   www.studioindiana.com

©2009, Printed in China

Publisher's Cataloging-in-Publication Data

Bower, John.

Journey's End: Relics and ruins of Indiana's transportation legacy /

photography by John Bower;

text by John Bower and Lynn Bower;

foreword by Brian Byrn.

p.   cm.

ISBN: 978-0-9745186-5-7

1. Transportation—History—Indiana—Pictorial works.

2. Vehicles—Indiana.

3. Indiana—Pictorial works.

4. Photography, Artistic.

I. Bower, John, 1949–.   II. Title.

TA1015.B69   2009

779.949772—dc22

Library of Congress Control Number: 2008911767

Dog n Suds advertising automobile (Constructed from
the front ends of two 1947 Crosleys in 1956. It remained operational
until 1972.)—Lafayette, Tippecanoe Co. (868.14)

Foreword

When John Bower asked me to write a Foreword to *Journey's End*, several memories from my childhood (before I discovered the world of Art) came to mind. Like most young boys growing up in southern Indiana, the love of adventure came via vacations taken in the family car. Ours was a '61 Buick Le Sabre and, several times, its four doors took us to the Great Smoky Mountains where exotic brown bears roamed the roads, and morning fog shrouded switchback highways. My father would pull over in the mornings to cook on our Coleman camp stove, and the days began and ended with imaginative dreams of pioneers, Indians, and Daniel Boone. These images would appear to me again in the paintings of N.C. Wyeth and other Golden Age illustrators. There were many antique shops along the way to and from Tennessee, and it seemed like we stopped at every one. I had never read a *Saturday Evening Post*, but there, amidst all kinds of strange things from the past, were wonderful old books with pictures by marvelous artists—and the images stayed fervent in my mind until years later when I would see originals by those same artists.

Returning from those trips was always as much fun as going because, upon arriving home, I would continue my fantasy travels. My father, ever suspended in a realm of wanderlust, would pile us into his 1941 Willys Jeep and strike out for dried-up creek beds and deer paths in the Harrison-Crawford Forest. These trips became great four-wheel-drive adventures that reached long-forgotten places like Old Leavenworth and vanished towns like Cold Friday.

Meanwhile, back in civilized Corydon, I remember playing on the old Constitution Elm. I would stand on the bridge of the sandstone monument and bark out orders to the imaginary crew of my pirate ship. I'm sure those who passed by thought I was reenacting the signing of the Hoosier constitution in the First State Capitol, but little did they know I was swashbuckling my way past English frigates. That love of the ocean was fueled by one of those old books, and the black-&-white movies that played on our television.

So there I was—torn between the love of roaming the mountains and a desire to ply the Atlantic (which I saw on another vacation, this time to Myrtle Beach, South Carolina). I had to decide if I were going to travel by land or by sea! Because the only large body of water even close to me was the Ohio River, I knew I'd need transportation (and the permission of my parents) if I were ever going to get back to the ocean or mountains.

It took another twelve years before I would see the ocean again. But, during the interval, a myriad of important events happened. I discovered I could draw and, with that, I set out to render my way far and wide. Drawings of pirate ships, Conestoga wagons, trains, planes, and yes, even automobiles, carried me off.

I think a majority of young boys, when first learning to draw, scrawl out a hot rod. My images were influenced by my brother's adventures in that land of exotic metal and candy-apple paint—California. Len was twelve years older, and he left home to join the Navy just as I was turning six, and I pursued his example in my artistic imagination. I would draw Rat Finks, choppers, and copy anything I could find by the Great One—Ed "Big Daddy" Roth! I know

I wasn't alone, because a recent exhibition of "Kalifornia Kulture" played well to sold-out museum visitors all across the country. Even in southern Indiana, I was caught up in the surfing and hot-rod craze. But I knew one thing for sure. I needed to get out of there to find those like-minded custom hot rodders. And that's when it happened—I was given my first mini-bike. From then on, until I turned sixteen, I rode the back roads, along rolling red-clay hills, with a new sense of freedom. I thought, if only Daniel Boone, or his brother Squire, had one of these babies.

Other events occurred, along my path to puberty, that aroused my interest in both art and transportation. My parents took me to the Lanesville Air Show where (on a grass landing strip) I saw my first bi-wing stunt plane. Highway I-64 made travel to Louisville faster—but not as much fun as traveling down the hilly Floyds Knobs. Then, one day my brother returned home on leave, and purchased a new 1965 Mustang convertible. Wow! That was enough to send me into fantasy-filled dreams of travel all across America. After getting out of the Navy, he topped it with a 1968 Corvette! It was official. I would spend all my waking hours emulating that standard of chrome and speed.

After a succession of bicycles, mini-bikes, and motorcycles, my first car (a 1970 Monte Carlo) took me to the big city of Louisville where I'd cruise Fourth Street and the Frisch's Big Boy Drive-In. As I turned 18, I visited my first museum in that car—the J.B. Speed Art Museum. My abilities in drawing, and looking at the objects in that museum, gave me insight into other things that would be more important than acquiring custom wheels. Art became my salvation, and I put on hold the idea of driving a souped up, chrome-laden, cam-thumping street rod. For me, maximum velocity would be achieved though painting, drawing, and studies in Art history. Freedom would come from that inalienable right of the artist to exercise a sense of creativity inspired by the world.

I left home for the capital city of Indianapolis to attend Butler University, then came back south—to Indiana University Southeast in New Albany. There, I rekindled my love for art—and road-trips with friends and relatives back and forth to IU Bloomington. Ultimately, my first car would take me to Elkhart, where I live and work today.

My love of the ocean had not waned when I first saw Lake Michigan and the Indiana Dunes. I would exclaim that it was like a great inland sea, to the chuckles of those who knew it well. My sense that this place was magical was enhanced when I saw the paintings of Frank Dudley. His works, like those illustrations in the old books I saw so long ago, fired my imagination about the world, as well as the great diversity of Indiana. I traveled through Brown County and encountered the work of other early Indiana painters. I rediscovered my home state though the vision of those, and other, American artists. Paintings by Edward Hopper and black-&-white photographs by artists like Walker Evans invigorated my memories of things past, things changed. The subjects in those paintings and photographs seemed universal, yet familiar—much like the images of John Bower. They are universal because the artist extracts that imaginative part of the subject to give us an opportunity to exercise our memories and view them as extraordinary.

I traveled from Corydon, at one end of Indiana, to the very edge of Michigan, and Elkhart became my home. Elkhart was not as exotic as California but it was close to Chicago. I soon began to discover its great history as a transportation hub for the railroad, and its manufacturing of "mobile" homes. Most importantly, I would discover a place that would become my primary professional residence—the Midwest Museum of American Art. My studies in art delivered me to a locale I have called home for over 27 years. It has become a destination point, after many long journeys elsewhere, as my wife Lisa and I continue to travel by trains, planes, and automobiles—always applying an artistic eye, and an imaginative outlook that originated on those first trips in that '61 Buick. For us, Indiana (like John's photography), seems as exotic as many far-off places, because we call it home.

Brian Byrn
Curator of Exhibitions & Education
Midwest Museum of American Art, Elkhart, Indiana
December 2008

Introduction

For me, there's a difference between a trip and a journey. To use a photography analogy, it's like comparing a digital snapshot taken with a cell phone to an evocative and moving image by Ansel Adams. One is simple and basic; the other rich, memorable, satisfying.

Yet, my dictionary defines *journey* matter-of-factly, as "the act of traveling from one place to another." In other words, getting from Point A to Point B. That may be fine for Webster, but I like to think of a journey as an experience that moves the psyche or affects the emotions, as well as gets us from A to B. So, I place journey alongside words like pilgrimage, odyssey, and expedition, each of which conjures up far more imagery than a mere trip.

Of course, the ultimate journey is Life itself, and it often leads us in a direction that can't be foreseen. While we all start off at a personal Point A (our birth), there's no way to know precisely how, or when, we'll reach our ultimate Point B (our demise). Nor can we anticipate any of the detours and stops along the way.

There's an old, faded, color photograph of me taken shortly after my own Point A. I'm just a few months of age, cradled in my dad's arms, with my big sister, Marsha, standing next to us. We're posed in front of a 1946 Chevrolet sedan, which is a two-tone blue, and badly in need of a coat of wax. There's another photo, taken at the same time, showing Mom and Grandma Dowell standing in front of that same car, looking at it with obvious admiration. In those days, particularly in a small town like Fowler, Indiana, a car (even a three-year-old one, less-than-shiny)

was something special—almost as special as having a first son. It made the perfect backdrop for a photo of the new baby boy—me.

There's nothing about that early image that could predict photography in my future, but it is representative of how each of our lives is inextricably linked to transportation—especially here in a state known officially as the Crossroads of America. All of us, as we grow, from infancy to old age, take countless trips—riding a bus to and from school, commuting to work, driving to the grocery, traveling to meetings—but most of these trips are forgotten. However, a few are remarkable enough to be called journeys—and they stand out.

I remember several journeys from my childhood. There was a first train ride—behind a steam-belching, coal-burning locomotive—while I was still in kindergarten. And a plane ride with a salesman friend of Dad's. Once airborne, he let me take controls. I was about 11, and felt just like Sky King. I don't recall any specifics about the locomotive, or the airplane, but I can still feel the emotion and excitement. That's what this book is about—the journeys that stay with us because they were memorable—sometimes, even extraordinary.

A few years after our family moved to Lafayette, and ten years after my picture was taken in front of that '46 Chevy, Grandma Dowell gave me her Kodak box camera. It was a dinosaur—decades old at the time—but I was excited nevertheless. Right away, I rode my bicycle up to the J.B. Lische Drug Store, where I bought a roll of film. In two days, I dropped it off to be developed. When I returned, at the end of the week, to pick up my very first batch of photographs, I was disappointed—they just weren't very good. But I wasn't discouraged. I figured I needed a better camera. So, I bought a roll of film for my parent's much newer Brownie Hawkeye—which they hardly ever used—and took more pictures. Again, the quality was pretty bad. Now, I *was* discouraged.

For some reason, I've kept the negatives from those first two rolls of film for almost 50 years—despite their poor composition and lack-of-focus. They show relatives (some now deceased), the house we moved away from in 1963, my red-and-white 24" Huffy bicycle, and a push cart I put together out of scrap lumber and scrounged wagon wheels.

As the years passed, I put photography on hold, and turned my attention to transportation. I replaced my Huffy with a new 26" Schwinn that had a shiny chrome front fork with spring suspension. Then, in my early teens, I built a mini-bike out of ½" steel water pipe and a Briggs-and-Stratton lawn-mower engine. When it was finished, and painted Rust-Oleum blue, it didn't look half bad—and its 1½-horsepower propelled me along just fine. As I rode it all over town, I started thinking about putting together my own automobile.

I was inspired by a series of articles in *Car Craft* magazine with the no-nonsense title, "How to Build a Hot Rod." Fortunately, the articles were well-written and easy-to-follow. It wasn't a project most boys would consider tackling, but I made my way through axles and suspension, brakes and steering, engine and transmission, then electrical wiring, learning how each component worked—repairing, rebuilding, and repainting wherever necessary. As I prepared for my senior year of high school, I completed the construction process, and painted it Ford Mustang Poppy Red—a stand-out bittersweet orange.

As I hack-sawed, drilled, sanded, filed, and welded, I borrowed my parent's camera again—they'd upgraded to an Instamatic—and took snapshots of my car's progress.

Sadly, my photographic skills were not improving. I was, at the time, a hands-on, left-brain sort of kid who preferred math, physics, and drafting courses, rather than history and Latin. Art and literature were outside my sphere of interest. But I was still interested in taking pictures so, after entering Purdue, I contacted a photography instructor in the Art department, to see if I could take his class. He was polite, but firm. The course was only open to Art majors, and I wasn't one.

Shortly after college, Lynn and I met, got married and, after a few years, bought a decrepit 1850's Federal-style farmhouse on the outskirts of Lafayette. About midway through the renovation, when we were in our late twenties, we purchased a used 35-mm Minolta camera. We took it along on day trips to Chicago, and elsewhere. But we primarily used it to photograph Lynn's artwork, and to document the restoration of our old house. I had fun with that camera, and my pictures were getting somewhat better, but they still weren't anything noteworthy.

For the next major stage of our journey through life, Lynn and I decided to put our newly restored farmhouse on the market, and relocate to Bloomington. Our decision was baffling to friends and relatives but, on the very day we painted the last wall, we called up a Realtor, and the house was sold within 24 hours.

The idea of moving to Bloomington wasn't completely out-of-the-blue. In fact, it had been in our thoughts for several years. When we'd honeymooned at the big yellow-brick hotel in French Lick (It was a Sheraton back then.), we'd fallen in love with the wooded hills of southern Indiana and, in particular, with Bloomington. Its large liberal-arts university and casual, arty atmosphere just felt right to us.

We had no job prospects in Bloomington, and knew no one there, so my left-brained self wasn't involved with the decision, but an emerging right-brained part of me was. In short, Lynn and I simply trusted that Destiny would lead the way—and it did. After a few years in Bloomington, we became full-time authors, wrote several books on building healthy houses and living healthy lifestyles—and we founded a successful small publishing business. Then, as we reached our 50s, we grew restless, and were ready to explore new horizons once again.

The next leg of our journey began when I picked up a flyer listing classes at Bloomington's John Waldron Art Center, and a photography course caught my eye. It was very basic, just eight weeks long, but I signed up, and was immediately hooked. Within days of completing the class, I purchased a new, medium-format Mamiya camera and started building my own darkroom. I also embarked on an in-depth, self-study program by reading every photography book I could get my hands on—monographs, histories, biographies, as well as books on technique. Within a few years I had over 300 books in my personal photography library.

From the day Lynn and I met, we've gone for drives together out in the country. Three or four times a month we'd head off in a direction we'd never been before, just to see what was there. Now, we found ourselves heading out—specifically to take photographs—two or three times a week. As I got used to my new camera, I was surprised to see that I was actually mastering the medium. I progressed from having one or two keepers per roll of film, to several. My darkroom skills also improved and, as I learned to access my creative side, I realized I'd probably had a latent ability all along.

One day, while we were out driving, Lynn suggested we publish a book of my photographs. Because we already owned our own publishing company, it seemed like an obvious next step. Just 8 years after taking that short photography course, we're completing this, our sixth Indiana photography book. It's been a journey neither of us could have foreseen ten years earlier, much less when we met in 1972.

Today, we lead lives completely intertwined with how we earn a living. Together, we travel highways and back roads, seeking out relics of a disappearing Hoosier past. As I take photographs, Lynn keeps records of the locations on her iMac laptop computer, and interviews fascinating local people. Together, we evaluate contact sheets to determine which images to print and, with her artist's eye (she has a degree in Art Education) she does an excellent job of critiquing my work. When it's time to prepare a book for the printer, she's the one who makes the final selection of images, as she designs and lays out the cover and all the pages.

So far, our books have required 75,000 miles of journeying, and we've visited every city and town (2,099 localities in all) on the Indiana Highway Map. By keeping our own hours, we can, on a minute's notice, set out on a 16-hour day trip. Or, I might spend time in my darkroom, while Lynn writes an essay about an interesting place we've investigated. Or, we might hike in the woods, or read a book. It's a job—a life—that suits us perfectly.

As we travel across Indiana, Lynn and I often marvel at how fortunate we are to be able to do what we do—driving around, exploring, discovering unique places. When we come across the battered and rusted hulk of a once-shiny Packard, we know it's much more than an abandoned car, for it was probably an important part of someone's life. When we see a stretch of heavy, steel railroad tracks being ripped up, when we look at the ruin of a limestone lock on the Wabash & Erie Canal, when we encounter an empty railroad station, we know these are places that have shaped the destinies of countless Hoosiers.

Yes, we all have memories of journeys involving cars, trains, buses, bridges, roads, and more. We remember how they affected us, changed our lives. There are tales of transportation journeys that all of us could tell but, with the passing of time, many of the stories are destined to be lost, forgotten, unrecorded. This book is filled with transportation relics, but it's not the objects that are important. It's the journeys they took us on—especially to destinations within ourselves. It's the journeys that make us who we are.

May *Journey's End* trigger memories of your sojourns across this Hoosier state—and keep them alive.

John Bower

0-6-0T Narrow Gauge (1,000 mm) Steam Locomotive, manufactured by H.K. Porter, 1928 (Louisville Cement Co. #13)—
Thresherman's Park, near Boonville, Warrick Co. (816.02)

2-8-4 Steam Locomotive, manufactured by Lima Locomotive Works, 1944 (New York, Chicago & St. Louis "Nickel Plate" Railroad #765)—
Ft. Wayne Historical Railroad Society, near New Haven, Allen Co. (858.10)

Jim Gardener's Filling Station—Livonia, Washington Co. (749.04)

Jacobi's Service Station—Galena, Floyd Co. (750.04)

Ford Truck Body—rural LaPorte Co. (850.06)

Diamond T Delivery Truck—rural Tippecanoe Co. (853.02)

Overpass (Pennsylvania Railroad)—Lebanon, Boone Co. (852.13)

Biplane and Dirigible (Limestone building detail)—Indianapolis, Marion Co. (837.01)

Dirigible (Limestone building detail)—Evansville, Vanderburgh Co. (815.12)

Darwin Ferry (The last ferry operating on the Wabash River, originally founded in 1818.)——near Darwin (Illinois), crossing to rural Vigo Co. (876.05)

East Pier Lighthouse and Catwalk (1904)—Michigan City, LaPorte Co. (828.12)

Forgotten Electric Railways

Massive steam locomotives belching black smoke. That's what comes to mind for most Hoosiers when they think about Indiana's railroad history. However, there was once an extensive railway network along which small cars, powered by electricity, darted. Because they connected cities and towns, "inter-city" was one of the first terms used to describe them. But, soon, they were universally known as *interurbans*.

The interurban railways were primarily passenger lines, although they sometimes carried freight as well. The very first companies were established in the late 1800s, with others getting into the business during the following several decades. The self-propelled cars ran on tracks and used electric motors powered by overhead wires.

Nearly all Indiana's early interurban companies enjoyed a meteoric rise in popularity, with millions of passengers riding annually for both business and pleasure. Then—around the time of World War I, as automobiles became more popular—there began a slow decline. By the 1940s and early '50s, there were few interurbans left. Today, only one remains in operation—the popular South Shore Line, which runs across northwest Indiana, connecting South Bend with Chicago. The South Shore's tracks, as with most interurban companies, were built parallel to preexisting steam-railway rights-of-way. That's because land was cheaper alongside existing tracks, and the established steam lines had already been constructed on the most direct routes between towns.

Throughout Indiana, a great deal of infrastructure was built by the various interurban companies: large carbarns where trolleys were stored and serviced, coal-fired electric-generating plants, electrical substations, waiting shelters, and depots—as well as bridges, culverts, a system of poles and wires, and tracks. Today, only a few remnants remain, the most common are simple rectangular, brick, flat-roofed stations and substations, now used for other purposes. A few once-essential buildings and miscellaneous structures sit forlornly along rail-less rights-of-way—their proud heritage all but forgotten. And the hundreds of trolley cars? Only a handful have escaped the scrap pile, to be seen at a few railroad museums. John and I found two, disintegrating anonymously, in out-of-the-way woodlots.

Many pluses were associated with Indiana's interurbans. They were relatively inexpensive to operate, quiet, and non-polluting (except for the power plants themselves). The electrified cars accelerated much faster than their hulking steam counterparts, so they could zip quickly—like jackrabbits—between stations. But, because they couldn't offer the same degree of freedom as automobiles, they all but disappeared—from the landscape and from our memories.

Hoffman Substation (Indianapolis & Cincinnati Traction Co.)—rural Marion Co. (516.13)

Interurban Car—rural Brown Co. (870.05)

Marion/Empire Motor Car Co.—Indianapolis, Marion Co. (819.03)

Anco Windshield Wiper Factory—Valparaiso, Porter Co. (829.05)

Ligonier Carriage Co.—Ligonier, Noble Co. (775.15)

National Motor Vehicle Co.—Indianapolis, Marion Co. (816.15)

Premiere Motor(car) Manufacturing Co.—Indianapolis, Marion Co. (819.06)

Boxcar (Louisville, New Albany & Corydon Railroad)—Indiana Railway Museum, French Lick, Orange Co. (884.14)

Boxcar (New York, Chicago & St. Louis "Nickel Plate" Railroad)—Indiana Transportation Museum, Noblesville, Hamilton Co. (879.13)

Interurban Bridge Piers (Union Traction Co.)—near Logansport, Cass Co. (868.01)

Interurban Substation #6 during the spring flood of 2008 (Indianapolis, Columbus & Southern Traction Co.)—Azalia, Bartholomew Co. (825.14)

Plymouth Automobile—near Mitchell, Lawrence Co. (805.06)

Ford Automobile—rural Morgan Co. (830.10)

Freight Depot (Pennsylvania Railroad, 1902)—Marion, Grant Co. (766.15)

Passenger Depot (Toledo, St. Louis & Western Railroad, 1903)——Veedersburg, Fountain Co. (870.04)

Passenger Depot (Pennsylvania Railroad, 1892) Moved from original location.——Frankton, Madison Co. (840.02)

Firebox, 0-6-0 Steam Locomotive, manufactured by American Locomotive Co., 1912 (New York Central Railroad #6894)—
Whitewater Valley Railroad, Connersville, Fayette Co. (823.07)

0-6-0 Steam Locomotive, manufactured by Baldwin Locomotive Works, 1907 (East Broad Top Railroad #6)—
Whitewater Valley Railroad, Connersville, Fayette Co. (823.09)

Ivan's Service

"Ivan's! Oh, you'll definitely want to check out Ivan's. It's a real time capsule." We'd heard similar enthusiastic statements from several people. So, intrigued, John and I set out on a hot July morning for Thorntown to meet Ivan's son, Floyd.

Floyd Fairfield inherited his father's Marathon station after Ivan passed away in the 1980s. The old garage, once a thriving small-town enterprise, at the corner of Pearl and Main Streets, has been suspended in time ever since.

When we arrived, we found a two-story frame building, covered with yellow and white vinyl siding. However, the original windows, with their checked red paint, still hinted to the structure's true age. An impressive, wooden, cantilevered roof projected over the front door. Above it, an IVAN'S SERVICE sign was flanked by a pair of faded Coca-Cola advertising disks.

Floyd arrived only a couple of minutes after we did, quickly unlocked the glass-paneled front door, and began telling us about the building's history. It seems his dad had bought the place from the original owner, who had operated a harness shop. After pointing out some highlights we shouldn't miss, Floyd said we could stay as long as we liked, and take photographs of whatever interested us. With a, "Just lock the door when you leave," he left us, and

Ivan's Service—Thorntown, Boone Co. (739.10)

headed over to a nearby restaurant for a late breakfast with friends.

Standing alone, we slowly took the place in. It was musty, crowded, and jumbled—but it was a museum of one man's life, his livelihood, and an era now past. For 35 years Ivan had run his service station until he eventually retired to Florida. But even then, he returned each summer to repair bicycles and lawn mowers, until his death about 25 years ago. That's when the business closed for good.

Over the years, curious townsfolk had occasionally peered through the front windows—captivated by glimpses of what lay just out of reach on the other side. Not us. We'd been lucky. We'd been able to cross the threshold. We were inside.

As John and I looked around, we were overwhelmed by a treasure trove of early- and mid-20th-century car parts—a collection of miscellany of varying vintages and origins. In fact, Ivan's was so brimming with automobile paraphernalia, so filled with unexpected curiosities and oddities, it was difficult to focus on any one thing. How to proceed?

I decided to first concentrate on the structure itself. The main level had a dark, oily-brown, oak floor, with walls painted an institutional green, reminiscent of the 1940s

Ivan's Service—Thorntown, Boone Co. (741.11)

Ivan's Service—Thorntown, Boone Co. (740.08)

Ivan's Service (Storage area under hinged step.)—
Thorntown, Boone Co. (741.08)

Ivan's Service—Thorntown, Boone Co. (742.12)

and '50s. There was a large front room, with a smaller storage room, and a restroom with a Boys sign on its door. Down a few steps, at the very rear, was a concrete-floored garage area. A narrow wooden stairway lead to an upper level, and a less-inviting one descended into a dark cellar.

As I scanned the contents, wandering, exploring, John started shooting. I came across an ancient cash register (sans money) with Ivan's hat still hanging on a nearby hook. Along a wall, cabinets overflowed with a conglomeration of what-nots and odds-and-ends. I particularly liked a wheelchair-contraption-sculptural-thing with welded-on horseshoes, old engine parts, a chrome flip-down sandwich grill, and a mélange of other disparate components, including a car battery, parked in the center of the front room. Floyd had told us it was meant to be shocking—literally.

And then, there were the ubiquitous automobile parts. V-belts seemed particularly numerous, but there were also spark plugs, air filters, oil filters, gaskets, and other commonly needed bits and pieces—many in original packaging, with small items stored in glass screw-top jelly jars. I smiled at an ancient metal cabinet emblazoned with EVEREADY MAZDA AUTO LAMPS and two images of antiquated light bulbs. Inside, were scores of tiny lamps for cars out-of-production for a half century or more.

Ivan's Service—Thorntown, Boone Co. (742.04)

Other stand-outs in the main room included a large, red, Coca-Cola cooler, a metal box of ANCO windshield wipers, spare lawn-mower wheels, several American flags, and a selection of home-made wooden whirligigs. Less conspicuous was a stack of alphabetical letters, each around 12" high. It took me a minute to realize that, if laid out side by side, they'd spell MARATHON. Leaning nearby, was a straw broom with bristles worn to nubs. Ivan must have been a very thrifty man—it didn't look like anything had ever been thrown out.

After a while, we decided to check out the upstairs. John found the light switch and led, carefully toting his camera and tripod. There were more V-belts and gaskets hanging on the walls. A row of wooden shelving ran down the center of the room, loaded with more glass jars containing whatever Ivan felt he might need some day, and cans of something called Solventol. Boxes and boxes, that once held Bun can-

Ivan's Service—Thorntown, Boone Co. (741.01)

dy bars, were filled with receipts and paperwork from de-cades and decades of running the business. On the floor, were a pair of cylinder heads for an early Ford V-8, as well as the wheel-less frames of a bike and a unicycle.

Back downstairs, I looked again behind the dusty wood-and-glass counter that had been Ivan's command post. Ready for use, were at least three tattered fly swatters, a pair of greasy flashlights, and several dull pencils. Tacked to the front of a cabinet hung an official Ivan's Marathon Service calendar, complete with a miniature rendition of Da-Vinci's *Last Supper*. All its months had been torn off, except November and December 1967. Next to it, was a yellowed

Coca-Cola daily calendar, helpfully informing onlookers that the "current day" was December 14, 1974. Inches away, lay a worn phone book with spring flowers and May 1976 printed on its cover.

It was clear to us that Time had a different character, a different effect, a different way of functioning, inside Ivan's than in the rest of creation. This was confirmed for us on a most personal level. When we entered 100 Pearl Street, we thought we'd be here for 20 minutes or so. But as we stepped outside, and locked the door, John glanced at his wristwatch. "Lynn," he said slowly, with more than a bit of surprise in his voice, "we've been here for two hours."

Viaduct (Baltimore & Ohio Railroad, 1901) 1,080' long, 112' high—over Laughery Creek, rural Ripley Co. (824.12)

Viaduct (Indianapolis Southern Railroad, 1906) 880' long, 80' high—over Shuffle Creek at Lake Lemon, rural Monroe Co. (859.09)

38

Buick Automobile—rural Monroe Co. (836.08)

Chevrolet Automobile—rural Monroe Co. (836.05)

Coaling Tower (New York, Chicago & St. Louis "Nickel Plate" Railroad)—Frankfort, Clinton Co. (651.09)

Coaling Tower (Monon Railroad)—Lafayette, Tippecanoe Co. (675.11)

Coaling Tower (Chicago South Shore & South Bend Railroad)—
Michigan City, LaPorte Co. (752.07)

Coaling Tower (Chicago & Eastern Illinois Railroad, 1941)—Sullivan, Sullivan Co. (636.12)

Interurban Carbarn/Shop (Northern Indiana Power Co.)——Kokomo, Howard Co. (866.02)

Interurban Substation (Indianapolis, Columbus & Southern Traction Co.)—near Retreat, Jackson Co. (840.13)

Passenger Depot (Chicago, Milwaukee, St. Paul & Pacific Railroad, 1898) Moved from original location.—
Alert, Decatur Co. (825.05)

Freight Depot (Chicago & Eastern Illinois Railroad, 1912)—
Clinton, Vermillion Co. (706.14)

Passenger Depot (Pennsylvania Railroad, 1908)—Flora, Carroll Co. (854.08)

America's First Automobile?

Legend has it that Elwood Haynes came up with the concept for a horseless carriage back in 1889. After a few years of doing research, and considering various options, he hired two Kokomo brothers, Elmer and Edgar Apperson, to build him an automobile.

Working after hours in a local machine shop, the brothers Apperson earned 40¢ an hour for their efforts, which culminated in the unveiling of the Pioneer on July 4th 1894. Although a curious crowd gathered for a look-see, it took the *Kokomo Daily Tribune* eleven days before it published an article about the unusual public event—in which it described the new mechanical contrivance as a "queer-looking vehicle."

Does this mean Haynes was the creator of America's first automobile? Some experts say yes, although others argue the point. They bestow that venerable honor on the Duryea brothers, or men with less familiar names such as Selden, McClure, Lambert, Schloemer and Toepfer, or Nadig (but certainly *not* Henry Ford). It's a dispute that will probably never be resolved—but Haynes' autos did have hood ornaments imprinted with the words "America's First Car."

Haynes Automobile Co.—Kokomo, Howard Co. (865.15)

In any case, the one-horsepower Pioneer was definitely a hit. So, in 1896, a business partnership was formed between the idea man and the men who could turn those ideas into reality. Slowly, the Haynes-Apperson Automobile Company became successful.

Then, in 1901, Elwood and the Appersons decided, on friendly terms, to go their separate ways. The next year, Elmer and Edgar formed the Apperson Brothers Automobile Company. For a while (until 1904) Elwood kept the firm's original name. Thereafter, it was known simply as the Haynes Automobile Company.

The enterprises grew into multi-million-dollar operations, then each failed in the '20s. Eventually, in 1937, the Chrysler Corporation took over one of the old Haynes factories on Kokomo's south side, where it operated until 1965.

When I photographed the old factory in 2008, it was still occupied—somewhat ironically—by an automobile salvage company, Warren's Auto Parts. Inside, I found racks of used engines, wheels, and various other components, all from scrapped vehicles—warehoused in an aging car factory that had witnessed the exuberant ups, and dramatic downs, of a pioneering Indiana automobile industry.

Haynes Automobile Co.—Kokomo, Howard Co. (789.04)

Haynes Automobile Co.—Kokomo, Howard Co. (789.09)

Haynes Automobile Co.—Kokomo, Howard Co. (789.08)

Chevrolet Transmission Plant (Razed in 2007.)——Muncie, Delaware Co. (717.02)

Edsel Dealership Sign—Marion, Grant Co. (766.05)

Caboose Interior (Louisville & Nashville Railroad) —Thresherman's Park, near Boonville, Warrick Co. (816.05)

Caboose (Baltimore & Ohio Railroad)—Indiana Railway Museum, French Lick, Orange Co. (884.08)

Passenger Depot (Pennsylvania Railroad, 1902)—Richmond, Wayne Co. (059.10)

Passenger Depot (Lake Erie & Western Railroad, 1914)—Frankfort, Clinton Co. (854.11)

Ronnie Clement's Sunoco Station with International Harvester Pickup Truck—
Hardinsburg, Washington Co. (750.15)

Morton Garage, "Closed after 37 yr."—Morton, Putnam Co. (704.12)

Shultz Gas Station and Garage (Later a hardware store.)——Lancaster, Huntington Co. (767.07)

Woodie's Pure Oil Service Station (Originally a doctor's office with stable.)——Headlee, White Co. (782.09)

0-4-0T Steam Locomotive, manufactured by Vulcan Iron Works, 1924 (Southwestern Portland Cement Co. Railroad #11)—
Whitewater Valley Railroad, Connersville, Fayette Co. (823.14)

4-8-2 Steam Locomotive, manufactured by American Locomotive Co., 1940 (New York Central #3001)—
National New York Central Railroad Museum, Elkhart, Elkhart Co. (851.09)

Concrete Bridge (Cleveland, Cincinnati, Chicago & St. Louis Railroad, 1906) Believed to be haunted by an African-American construction worker who was buried in wet concrete during the bridge's construction.—over White Lick Creek, near Danville, Hendricks Co. (831.14)

Railroad Overpass (Southern Indiana Railway) Although a few concrete structures were built, work on this line was suspended on Christmas Day in 1905 after an expenditure of $447,714.—over Hog Creek, near Bowling Green, Clay Co. (087.05)

A Rochester Depot

As we entered Rochester, John said, "I've heard about a concrete water-tower base. It's supposed to be along one of the railroads, somewhere here in town."

Not knowing which track, we started following the first set we came across. We passed landmarks we'd photographed on previous excursions—the old feed store, the closed-up

Passenger/Freight Depot (Erie Railroad, 1892)—Rochester, Fulton Co. (864.07)

creamery—but saw no water-tower base. As we continued along the rails, I suddenly blurted, "Look!" Just up ahead was a depot we hadn't heard about. It was medium-sized, clapboard-covered, and constructed in the classic railroad-station style. It appeared abandoned. Remarkably, it's original doors and windows had not been boarded over.

Across the street, sat the concrete water-tower base we'd been searching for. Oddly, it was stranded in the backyard of a house—impressively tall and massive, with an unusual diagonally planked entry door. We decided to check out the intriguing depot first.

Someone had installed a corrugated-metal roof and also given the outer walls a coat of pale-yellow and pearl-gray paint. Otherwise, it appeared that nothing had been cleaned up, repaired, or altered in any way. A "Rochester" sign still hung on one end of the building, and a rambling section for handling freight was attached to the other. An exuberance of weeds grew in the cracked pavement.

Surprisingly, the entry door was ajar, so I pushed it open. Why hadn't this old building been secured? From among the uneven mass of discolored detritus and debris on the floor, a small piece of white paper caught my eye—a blank Lackawanna Railroad Inspection Sheet from the early '70s. Was that when the station was last inspected? Or, when it was shut down?

The wood-trimmed ticket counter was still there—cluttered and badly deteriorated. A heavy, cast-iron heater was firmly planted in the lobby. As I stood, taking it all in, I could imagine early-morning passengers gratefully huddling around the radiator, in this cozy, public space.

I proceeded gingerly through the rest rooms, a station manager's room and, in the rear, the freight-handling area. Back there, I spotted a weighty, mechanical contrivance in a half-opened, pine shipping crate. What was it? Why was it still here? Had the station closed before it could be shipped, or

Water Tower Base (Erie Railroad)— Rochester, Fulton Co. (864.10)

had it arrived and gone unclaimed? One thing was for certain—this was a place of more questions than answers.

Passenger/Freight Depot (Erie Railroad, 1892)——Rochester, Fulton Co. (863.12)

"Elsie B" Ohio River Tow Boat (51.4' long, 16.5' wide, 400 hp, built 1979)—near Madison, Jefferson Co. (841.08)

"Lady B" Ohio River Tow Boat (41' long, 19.9' wide, 600 hp, built 1976)——near Madison, Jefferson Co. (841.15)

Ritner Tunnel, also known as the "Big Tunnel" (Baltimore & Ohio Railroad, 1857) 1,731' long—near Ft. Ritner, Lawrence Co. (881.09)

Patton Tunnel (Southern Railroad, 1882) 769' long—
near Taswell, Crawford Co. (811.09)

Barton Tunnel (Southern Railroad, 1907) 2,217' long—
rural Orange Co. (885.03)

Duncan Tunnel (Southern Railroad, 1881) 4,295' long—
Edwardsville, Floyd Co. (812.08)

Willow Valley Tunnel (Baltimore & Ohio Railroad, c.1901) 1,160' long—
near Willow Valley, Martin Co. (885.11)

Horseman's Group Meeting House (Built in the 1920s.)——Peoria, Miami Co. (796.01)

Wagon Wheels—rural Harrison Co. (212.09)

Roundhouse (New York, Chicago & St. Louis "Nickel Plate" Railroad)—Frankfort, Clinton Co. (709.15)

Roundhouse (Southern Railroad)—Princeton, Gibson Co. (531.03)

Plymouth Automobile—rural Monroe Co. (834.06)

Chevrolet Automobile—near New Albany, Floyd Co. (843.12)

Dodge Automobile—near Mitchell, Lawrence Co. (803.11)

Demolishing Studebaker

Over 200 different manufacturers have produced automobiles and trucks in Indiana over the last 100-plus years. Some companies came and went quickly, a few lasted for

Studebaker Corp. (Gate House)—
South Bend, St. Joseph Co. (806.08)

decades. Familiar names include Deusenberg, Auburn, Apperson, Marmon—and Studebaker. Known for its distinc-

tive styling and state-of-the-art innovations, the Studebaker Corp. unveiled its first car in 1911, and its last rolled off an assembly line in 1966.

Studebaker Corp. (top of Building 72)—
South Bend, St. Joseph Co. (683.11)

Today, very little of Studebaker's South Bend facility remains. I was drawn to photograph the 125-acre industrial complex on three different occasions. On my first visit, some of the colossal concrete buildings were in the process of being razed. It was obvious they'd been built to last, and the demolition process appeared to be difficult and time consuming. However, when I returned a few months later, I found an expansive, barren, gravel lot.

Building 78 (at right and page 74) disappeared just a few weeks after I shot it. It had once housed a press-room die shop, frame-assembly line, engineering department, and tool room. As I walked through the cavernous space, I could imagine the activity, the noise, the overhead crane loading railroad cars and transferring material to the various floors. Building 85 (below)—which has, so far, escaped the wrecking ball—was the foundry, with a capacity of pouring 400 tons of metal every day.

Studebaker Corp. (Building 85, Foundry)—South Bend, St. Joseph Co. (807.01)

Studebaker Corp. (Building 78)——South Bend, St. Joseph Co. (682.14)

I have a subtle family connection to Studebaker because, when he was in his 20s, my dad sold Studebakers for a short time in Texas. It wasn't his calling and, after a few months, he returned to Indiana and went on to other endeavors.

While Dad never owned a new one, he did purchase a used bullet-nosed Studebaker in the mid-1950s for my mom to drive. Second cars were rare back then, but it was well worn, and didn't cost him much—just $100. We all called it a puddle-jumper. It only lasted for a year, but Dad seemed to think he'd gotten his money's worth for 12 months of transportation for the wife and kids, so he bought another one—also for $100. After the third, Mom got an inexpensive new vehicle.

I remember those old cars with affection—particularly their characteristic prows—and how we all piled into them to go to school, run errands, or visit the doctor. So, it pleased me get some photographs of the very factory where they'd been built so long ago—before it disappeared, just like a certain trio of puddle-jumpers.

Studebaker Corp. (Building 78)—South Bend, St. Joseph Co. (682.05)

Studebaker Corp. (Demolition of Buildings 79 and 82)—South Bend, St. Joseph Co. (683.08)

Buggy Repair Shop (Later Bill Meyers Garage.)——Plevna, Howard Co. (796.07)

Merom Livery—Merom, Sullivan Co. (786.12)

Sam's Truck Stop—rural Hamilton Co. (796.11)

Alexander's Sit-N-Bull Diner—near Monroe, Tippecanoe Co. (852.15)

Ford Truck—rural Morgan Co. (831.07)

Packard Automobile—rural Monroe Co. (836.07)

Stable (Evansville Brewery Association)—Evansville, Vanderburgh Co. (814.13)

Stable (Pearl Laundry)—Evansville, Vanderburgh Co. (814.15)

Shrader Stables—New Albany, Floyd Co. (727.02)

Gordon's or Millville's Lock #24 (Whitewater Canal)——near Metamora, Franklin Co. (821.01)

Hydraulic Concrete Aqueduct and Waste Weir (Whitewater Canal)——Connersville, Fayette Co. (824.01)

Indiana Harbor and Ship Canal (Connects the Grand Calumet River with Lake Michigan, construction began in 1901.)——East Chicago, Lake Co. (828.05)

Passenger Depot (Lake Shore & Michigan Southern Railroad and Baltimore & Ohio Railroad, 1910)—Gary, Lake Co. (689.13)

Passenger Depot (Pennsylvania Railroad, 1902)—Richmond, Wayne Co. (716.09)

A Startling Sight

A mammoth, streamlined, aluminum snout loomed out of the foliage, pointing straight toward State Road 54. John and I gasped as we drove by. We were near Dugger, in western Greene County, on a photo trip for our third book, *Second Stories*, when we spotted the derelict Amtrak engine just yards from the highway. Because we didn't have time to stop and shoot it that day, I made a note of the location. We knew we'd come back someday.

But someday didn't arrive until a few years later, when we were working on this book, our sixth. Finally, on a sunny September morning, we returned. John pulled into the gravel drive between the once-startling engine and two Amtrak cars that were less visibly threatening, and stopped. A man walked towards our Pontiac Vibe. He turned out to be Ted Monier, owner of this place—Ted Monier Parts and Salvage. Ted was a distinctive-looking fellow with a long beard, wearing an aging hat with his company's name embroidered on the front.

Amtrak Engine—rural Greene Co. (874.05)

Amtrak Car—rural Greene Co. (874.11)

When we asked how the engine and cars got here, Ted explained that the former owner of his salvage yard once had a contract to scrap retired rolling stock at Amtrak's Beech Grove repair facility. Because he thought they'd make interesting storage buildings or cottages, he trucked six of them down here about 20 years ago. Since then, one was sold for a river cabin, and two ended up being dismantled for scrap. That left the three we'd spotted. "Take as many photos as you want of them," he said, "just be careful."

Then, as an aside, he told us, "You know, you're not the first to take pictures of those old cars. Every so often, someone stops by to ask permission. Sometimes, a local photographer even uses them as a backdrop for high-school senior-class pictures."

Soon, John and I were eagerly investigating the once ultra-modern, fast-looking, cars. Sadly, their weather-worn metal skins were scratched and pock marked with bullet holes. Red-white-and-blue stripes, that used to race boldly along their sides, were now faded. Windows were cracked or missing. The interiors had been gutted. Adding to the dereliction, there was an exuberant overabundance of weeds and scrubby trees starting to engulf and swallow them up. All this made for great compositions. John took photo, after photo, after photo.

Amtrak Car—rural Greene Co. (874.10)

Amtrak Engine—rural Greene Co. (874.13)

Amtrak Engine—rural Greene Co. (874.09)

Tourist Cabins (On the National Road. Buildings are made of glazed tile.)—rural Hendricks Co. (477.12)

Cedar Crest Motel (Brick pavement is the remains of the original two-lane National Road.)——rural Putnam Co. (484.09)

Ford Truck—near Mitchell, Lawrence Co. (804.02)

Ford Automobile—near Mitchell, Lawrence Co. (805.15)

Automobile and Truck Graveyard—rural Jackson Co. (080.12)

Ford Thunderbirds—near Mitchell, Lawrence Co. (813.01)

Buick Automobile—Silverville, Lawrence Co. (159.13)

Automobiles used as erosion control—rural Johnson Co. (810.11)

Air Traffic Control Tower (Stout Field, closed in 1961)——Indianapolis, Marion Co. (817.06)

Airport Hanger (Jefferson Proving Ground, closed in 1995)—near Madison, Jefferson Co. (841.04)

Airport Hanger (McCordsville Airpark, later Brookside Airpark, closed in 2003)—
McCordsville, Marion Co. (833.11)

Shay, Three Truck, Narrow Gauge (36"), Geared Steam Locomotive, manufactured by Lima Locomotive Works, 1929
(New Mexico Lumber Co. Railroad #7)—Heston Steam Museum, Heston, LaPorte Co. (851.03)

2-8-2 Steam Locomotive, manufactured by Lima Locomotive Works, 1922
(New York, Chicago & St. Louis "Nickel Plate" Railroad #624)—Hammond, Lake Co. (827.06)

A Field of Hudsons

While John and I were driving down a lonely road one evening, I spotted, far out in a field, what looked like rusting automobiles. As I focused my gaze, I could tell that they were indeed old cars—perhaps Hudsons. This was exciting stuff, but the sun was setting, and it was too late to shoot anything this day, so I jotted down the address. We would definitely have to find our way back.

And we did, several weeks later. After pulling into the gravel drive, we quickly scanned the assemblage of corroded vehicles, camouflaged by snaking vines and scrubby weeds. They were Hudsons all right. Unfortunately, there was no one at the house to give us permission to photograph them. John wrote a note and tucked it in the screen door.

Field of Hudsons—somewhere in Indiana (837.12)

Field of Hudsons—somewhere in Indiana (838.11)

Field of Hudsons, somewhere in Indiana (838.06)

One way or another, we were determined to track down the owner.

Back in Bloomington, we waited a few days. With no response to his message, John began making phone calls, starting with the local library. Eventually, he talked to a relative of the owner who knew about the Hudsons and was able to supply a name and telephone number. With fingers crossed, John dialed, and explained our mission. Happily, he was told that, yes, he could take photographs—but only if the location remained a secret. The owner did not want the whereabouts of his cache of Hudsons to be revealed. John agreed.

How had I known they were Hudsons, from such a distance, under weeds, and in the duskiness of twilight? When I was a girl, my friend Rita's parents had one—a light-grayish-tan, swept-back Hornet. It resembled a large, pasty-looking beetle more than its svelte yellow-and-black namesake.

I have a fond memory of the time Rita's mom took her, my twin sister, Lee, and me to a local Fourth of July celebration in the odd-looking car. After we parked, we three girls were told we could sit on the Hudson's roof to watch the fireworks. At least that was the plan. We soon discovered that the rear of the car made a great slide. After a couple of trips down, we were told to stop. Lee and Rita did but,

Field of Hudsons—somewhere in Indiana (838.08)

Field of Hudsons—somewhere in Indiana (838.03)

unable to contain myself (even though I was repeatedly warned), I slid down that irresistibly slide-able rear end—over and over again. I was usually quite well-behaved, but I simply couldn't stop.

Rita's father had acquired the Hornet while working for Detroit's Hudson Motor Car Company. My Dad, too, had a job there at one time—as a young draftsman. On his last day, Dad took with him some blueprints of the drawings he'd been working on. Lee and I happened across them once—rolled up and hidden (but not quite well enough) in the basement—and asked him about them. He said they were designs for major engine innovations, ones that might even be revolutionary, but would never be realized. I could sense he was proud of what he'd worked on, yet a bit guilty about bringing it home. I never saw the blueprints again.

Now, John and I were standing in the midst of an entire overgrown field filled with Hudsons. But, it was more than just an unmowed back lot, it was a private resting place—an anonymous vehicular graveyard. Here were four long rows of Hudsons, neatly laid out for eternity, side-by-side, obviously placed with care some decades earlier. There were a variety of models—all Hudsons—including Wasps, Jets, Hornets, even a few Hudson trucks. Each was badly decomposed, some had missing parts, some had been in accidents. Most had succumbed to the ravages of Time, in the form of a cancer-like, reddish-orange oxidation. Thick, tangled layers of vegetation had become a shroud for many, nearly engulfing them, a protection from prying eyes—but not ours.

For over an hour we paid our respects, and photographed them. John used his medium-format film camera, while I used a small digital camera, to capture gap-toothed grilles, ravaged upholstery, broken windshields, and rusted bumpers. As we walked back to our shiny, salsa-red Vibe, pulling burrs and sticky seeds from our jeans, we talked about what a great find this had been. We spoke about how those Hudsons had once been show-room perfect—the pride of their owners. Now, they were bio-degrading, slowly turning to dust. I looked at John with a sudden disturbing thought, "You know, we're older than some of those cars."

Field of Hudsons—somewhere in Indiana (837.06)

Field of Hudsons—somewhere in Indiana (838.12)

Lock #47 (Wabash and Erie Canal)—near Riley, Vigo Co. (184.09)

Culvert (Carried the Whitewater Canal over City Run Creek.)——Milton, Wayne Co. (845.08)

Roundhouse (Southern Railroad)—Princeton, Gibson Co. (530.13)

Air Compressor, Roundhouse (Southern Railroad)—Princeton, Gibson Co. (530.15)

Engine House (New Jersey, Indiana & Illinois Railroad, 1920s) Owned by the Singer Manufacturing Co.—
South Bend, St. Joseph Co. (808.06)

Fort Wayne Street Bridge, also known as the Indiana Avenue Bridge (Indiana Electric Railway Co., 1897) Used for automobile traffic today.—
over the Elkhart River, Goshen, Elkhart Co. (852.03)

Water Tower Base (Erie Railroad)——Decatur, Adams Co. (754.13)

Interurban Passenger/Freight Depot (Fort Wayne & Northern Indiana Traction Co.)—Delphi, Carroll Co. (855.07)

Interurban Passenger Depot and Substation (Union Traction Co., c.1913)—Springport, Henry Co. (833.08)

Interurban Powerhouse (Union Traction Co.)—LaFontaine, Wabash Co. (839.05)

Chevrolet Automobile—rural Monroe Co. (835.06)

Ford Truck—near Mitchell, Lawrence Co. (804.07)

Passenger Depot (Erie Railroad, 1883)—Monterey, Pulaski Co. (783.07)

Passenger Depot (Pennsylvania Railroad, 1894)—Greencastle, Putnam Co. (878.01)

Winona's Interurban Railway

Lynn and I were driving along the north shore of Winona Lake, just outside Warsaw. As we went under some raised railroad tracks, I knew we'd found what we were after—Powerhouse #2 of the Winona Interurban Railway. From here, electricity had been generated to power a passenger railway that once ran from Warsaw, up to Goshen, and down to Peru.

We parked, and walked up to the still-impressive brick building. Although long abandoned, I'd seen a floor plan in a book about Indiana's interurbans at our public library, so I could visualize what had once been. Four gigantic coal-fired boilers had dominated most of the large main room. To one side was a coal shed, to the other, a generator room. Water had been pumped into the boiler room through a 36"-diameter wooden pipe, which had its intake 200' out in Winona Lake.

The steam generated here turned two 750-hp Allis Chalmers stationary steam engines, each of which was coupled to a 2,300-volt generator. Transformers stepped-up the electrical potential to 33,000 volts.

Powerhouse #2 (Winona Interurban Railway)—Warsaw, Kosciusko Co. (862.07)

Such high voltage was needed to force electrons through an expansive grid of high-tension wires out to a series of substations. Located at intervals along the railroad's right-of-way, each substation was equipped with step-down transformers to reduce the voltage to a lower, more appropriate level for the electrical wires suspended above the tracks. Using a single, roof-mounted, hinged arm, an interurban car could maintain a secure connection to its overhead power source, in order to run its motor.

Founded in 1902, the Winona Interurban Railway was never very profitable. In 1907, it carried an average of over 1,000 people a day. By 1934, less than 300 a day were using the system. Still, it survived until 1952, when operations finally ceased. In 1971, the powerhouse's landmark 175'-tall brick chimney was toppled. For a while, the old building was home to a business called Gatke Corp., but it eventually moved out.

When Lynn and I explored the rundown site, we found no evidence of the deteriorating structures' original purpose—except for (possibly) a pair of large knife switches (left). The steam engines, coal conveyors, generators, transformers, tracks—all were gone. I was grateful for the information I'd come across at the library. Without it, like most Hoosiers, I would never have known about this place, nor all that had occurred here not so long ago.

Generator Room, Powerhouse #2 (Winona Interurban Railway)—Warsaw, Kosciusko Co. (863.01)

Boiler Room, Powerhouse #2 (Winona Interurban Railway)—Warsaw, Kosciusko Co. (862.10)

Bob's Service Center (Besides purchasing gasoline and groceries here, you could also visit with
Chico, Bob's pet monkey.)——Argos, Marshall Co. (783.10)

Willis F. Byrne Filling Station (1940), Clyde Worman Filling Station (1950)——Evansville, Vanderburgh Co. (712.11)

Jonesy's Standard Oil Service Station—Lafayette, Tippecanoe Co. (869.02)

Ringham's Pure Oil Service Filling Station—
Indianapolis, Marion Co. (705.02)

Huber's Standard Oil Service Station—Freetown, Jackson Co. (696.10)

0-4-2T Steam Locomotive, manufactured by H.K. Porter, 1913 (Coronet Phosphate Co. Railroad #6)—
Hoosier Valley Railroad Museum, North Judson, Starke Co. (829.15)

0-6-0 Steam Locomotive, manufactured by American Locomotive Co., 1912 (New York Central Railroad #6894)—
Whitewater Valley Railroad, Connersville, Fayette Co. (823.04)

Wade Tower (Chesapeake and Ohio Railroad)—
near Lacrosse, LaPorte Co. (829.11)

Hohman Avenue Tower (Lake Shore & Michigan Southern, Indiana
Harbor Belt, Nickel Plate, Monon, and Erie Railroads, 1900)—
Hammond, Lake Co. (828.04)

Union City Tower (Cleveland, Cincinnati, Chicago & St. Louis Railroad)—
Union City, Randolph Co. (770.14)

Watson Tower (Baltimore & Ohio, Pennsylvania, and Southern Indiana
Railroads)—Watson, Clark Co. (842.09)

Walkerton Tower (Baltimore & Ohio Railroad)—Walkerton, St. Joseph Co. (849.11)

Covered Bridge (Built by A. M. Kennedy & Sons in 1881. Floated off its foundation in an 1892 flood into this field, where it has been used as a barn ever since.)——near Homer, Rush Co. (845.03)

Covered Bridge (At 434' in length, this is the longest Covered Bridge in the United States. Built in 1875 by J. J. Daniels, and taken out of service in 1970.)——over the East Fork of the White River, near Medora, Jackson Co. (844.08)

Lincoln Automobile—rural Monroe Co. (836.01)

Lincoln Continental Automobile—rural Morgan Co. (870.15)

Murl May's Garage

"A guy emailed me about a business in Salamonia that's supposed to look like it did when it closed decades ago," John remarked, while driving. "I think we've got time to check it out before we find a place to eat."

Jay County's Salamonia was like many small Indiana towns—it had seen better days, but there were still people around who called it home. Because there were few commercial buildings, we had no trouble finding the defunct garage/gas station on a corner lot. It was an aged structure with dingy white clapboards and a rambling roof above a pair of primordial gas pumps. It was our kind of place.

While John set up his camera and tripod, I peered through the dusty front window where the words "Murl May" had been carefully painted long ago on the glass. "It's really packed inside," I eagerly reported. "Why don't you see if you can find someone to let us in," John suggested, nodding his head toward the nearby houses.

As I stood on the porch of a home behind the station, looking through the screen door, I saw only an empty front room. After ringing the doorbell, a man's voice answered from deep within, "Come in," it beckoned. "But I'm a stranger!" I countered. "Come in. Come in anyway," the voice encouraged. I entered hesitantly.

A spry old gentleman with a cane walked into the living room. "Do you know who owns the place next door?" I inquired. "Well, I do," he answered cheerfully. After he introduced himself as Paul May, I explained what we were doing, and asked if he could show us the garage sometime. With a twinkle in his eye he replied, "How about now?"

As I strode back to John and told him the good news, one of the wooden garage doors suddenly slid to the side. There stood Paul, beaming, next to a handsome 1925 Buick roadster. This garage, he said, had been his father's.

Paul explained that his dad had started the business back in 1912 or '13, and operated it until his death in 1962. According to Paul's younger brother Ralph (whom we met a few months later) in order to make ends meet during the Depression, their dad also sold generators, did plumbing and electrical work, installed windmills, and repaired wa-

Murl May's Garage—Salamonia, Jay Co. (756.11)

ter wells. Paul was a farmer, living out in the county, when Murl passed on, while Ralph and their sister had settled in Anderson. None were interested in moving back to Salamonia to take over their father's enterprise. So, the garage was locked up and left as it was. Later, after his mother died, Paul said he and his wife decided to move back into town—into the May family home, adjacent to the garage, which continued to remain closed.

As John and I entered, we knew at once we were in an untouched, cluttered, yet fascinating, depository of 20th-century history. English ivy had invaded the interior and was growing over one of the counters. It added a mystical quality to it all. Piles and piles of who-knew-what lay on every surface. This was an archaeologist's dream.

Murl May's Garage—Salamonia, Jay Co. (756.05)

Murl May's Garage—Salamonia, Jay Co. (757.04)

Murl May's Garage—Salamonia, Jay Co. (757.15)

I picked up an advertising flyer from a stack. It depicted a happy "modern" family sitting around a console radio. The text proclaimed that such a wondrous happening could be a reality for anyone who electrified their house—with a Delco home generator. A pile of posters advertised the latest movie. It starred Charlie Chaplin. Except for the grimy top sheets, this stuff looked as if it was printed yesterday. And, it was everywhere.

Along one wall sat shelves of glass-encased batteries amid a strange configuration of switches and pointy-topped light bulbs. Paul said it was a system his father had devised for recharging car batteries. There were wooden cabinets, packed with car parts for vehicles that were now antiques. I spotted a framed mirror with two sets of women's legs painted on it. "What's this," I asked. "Oh, that's for Nehi soda pop," Paul said. I looked closely at the silk stockings, black pumps, and the bit of flirty skirt above the knees. I could just make out the faded letters N-E-H-I superimposed over the dismembered limbs. "Nehi, like

knee-high," Paul laughed, tapping his leg.

There was also a 1914 Model T touring car, and a blue 1953 Packard which, other than needing a little wax, appeared to be in great shape. "Open the door and check out the interior," Paul urged. Although it was a bit musty, the striped upholstery was almost pristine. "This Packard was sure easier to park in here than the Cadillac I've got now," he mused. I looked over at his current means of transport, and was amazed it could be maneuvered into the garage at all.

When we all stepped outside, I saw Paul attempting to close the sliding garage door. "This one sticks, so I might need a little help with it. You see, I'm 92 now." Together, he and I pushed the heavy stubborn door into place. "I can do the rest myself," he said, shooing me off good naturedly. With good-bye waves, John and I pulled away and headed off to find dinner. Murl May's Garage had been an excellent adventure, and Paul an excellent guide.

Murl May's Garage—Salamonia, Jay Co. (757.09)

Murl May's Garage—Salamonia, Jay Co. (756.13)

Tulip Trestle Viaduct (Indianapolis Southern Railroad, 1906) 2,800' long, 175' high. This is the third longest bridge of its kind in the world.——over Richland Creek, rural Greene Co. (873.14)

Swing Bridge (Illinois Central Railroad) One of several movable railroad bridges connecting Indiana and Illinois. This section rotated to allow river traffic to pass.——over Wabash River, near Griffin, Gibson Co. (871.06)

Bascule Bridge (New York, Chicago & St. Louis "Nickel Plate" Railroad, c.1910) A type of drawbridge,
most of the lifting mechanism has been removed except for the curved roller track.——
over Grand Calumet River, Hammond, Lake Co. (827.14)

Raised Viaduct (Louisville & Nashville Railroad, 1932) Three miles long. Ohio River bridge in background.——
near Rahm, rural Vanderburgh Co. (814.08)

Rail Diesel Car (RDC-3), a self-propelled diesel/hydraulic passenger/baggage car with stainless-steel body, manufactured by Budd Company, 1954
(Chicago & North Western Railroad #430)—Indiana Railway Museum, French Lick, Orange Co. (884.07)

E8 Diesel-Electric Locomotive, 2,250 hp., manufactured by General Motors Electro-Motive Division, 1953 (New York Central Railroad #4085)—
National New York Central Railroad Museum, Elkhart, Elkhart Co. (851.12)

Art Deco Greyhound Bus Station (Built in 1938, closed in 2007)—Evansville, Vanderburgh Co. (791.08)

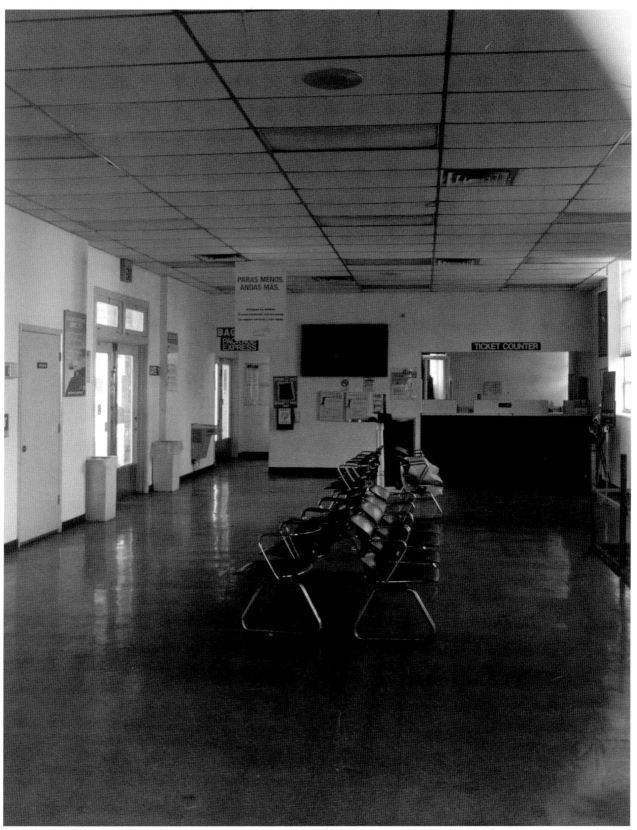

Art Deco Greyhound Bus Station (Interior was photographed one month after the station closed.)——Evansville, Vanderburgh Co. (791.10)

Caboose (Baltimore & Ohio Railroad)—Indiana Railway Museum, French Lick, Orange Co. (884.09)

Passenger Car (Chicago Transit Authority Railroad) Was used on the "El" in Chicago and its suburbs.⸺
Indiana Transportation Museum, Noblesville, Hamilton Co. (879.04)

Ford Truck—near Dillsboro, rural Dearborn Co. (808.13)

Graham Brothers Truck (Manufactured in Evansville.)—Windfall, Tipton Co. (860.02)

Stone Head Road Marker (Carved by H. Cross in 1851.)—rural Brown Co. (844.11)

Afterword

When we were driving around southern Indiana for our first photography book, *Lingering Spirit*, six years ago, Lynn suggested we ought to do our next one on transportation. To which I responded, "I don't think there would be much to photograph." So, we worked on other books, with other themes. And, as we worked on them, I came to see what a good idea she'd had—and how varied such a book could be.

As we started to really get into this project, we found not only relics and ruins of automobiles and trucks (and service stations and garages), but the remains of canals, railroads, interurbans, riverboats, even airports. I'd always known, of course, that, in time, vehicles rust and wear out—then they're usually junked for scrap. And, that their infrastructure—factories, depots, canal locks, railroad bridges—eventually get sold, reused, or torn down. But what truly surprised me was how much remained—how much

Full-size, authentic reproduction of the Wright *Flyer*—
Wilbur Wright Birthplace, near Millville, Henry Co. (886.15)

had simply been walked away from, to sit idle, derelict, and nearly forgotten. In the end, we discovered so much related to Indiana's transportation heritage, that we had

more images to sort through than for any previous book we've done.

For me, two Hoosiers, whose combined lives spanned a mere century, illustrate the many changes transportation has undergone in Indiana's brief history—Wilbur Wright and Gus Grissom.

In 1867, just two years after Jules Verne wrote *From the Earth to the Moon*, Wilbur Wright was born near Millville, Indiana in a tiny farmhouse on a little-traveled, rutted, dirt road. At the time, Indiana's canals were becoming passé, and railroads were expanding, yet most Hoosiers still traveled on foot, or relied on animal power. As a young man, when the very first horseless carriages were being built by hand, Wilbur, along with his brother Orville, envisioned an even more amazing means of transport—the flying machine.

Orville Wright was a high-school dropout. Wilbur completed his required courses, but moved with his family to Ohio so abruptly he never received his diploma. Despite lacking college educations, the brothers made detailed studies of all aspects of flight. They closely watched how birds flew, experimented with wing configurations, and built their own wind tunnel to test airfoil designs. In 1903—only two years after H.G. Wells' *The First Men on the Moon* was published—the Wrights made the world's first controlled, powered, and sustained heavier-than-air flight. It lasted only twelve seconds, but it changed everything. It would be another 5 years before Henry Ford unveiled his Model T.

In 1926, only 14 years after Wilbur's death, Gus Grissom was born in Mitchell, Indiana. In that same year Robert Goddard launched the world's first liquid-fueled rocket. Gus grew up in an era when interurbans were still running in parts of Indiana—but automobiles were much more common. After graduating from Purdue University, he joined the military, and became a pilot at age 25. He witnessed the evolution of air travel from propeller-driven planes to supersonic jets.

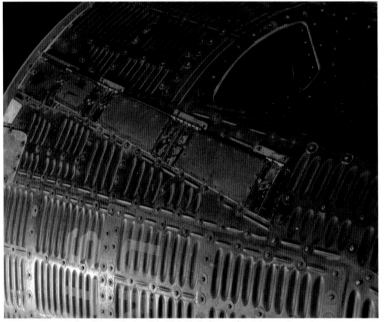

Gus Grissom's (unsinkable) *Molly Brown* Gemini capsule— Spring Mill State Park, near Mitchell, Lawrence Co. (881.13)

As one of NASA's original seven Mercury astronauts, Gus Grissom helped usher in the Space Age. In 1961, he became the second American to enter space and, three years later, he commanded the first manned Gemini flight. Tragically, he was killed in a fire during a 1967 training exercise, for what was to be the first manned Apollo mission. Shortly thereafter, the Apollo program succeeded in putting a man on the moon—an accomplishment that, previously, had been the subject of Wells' and Verne's science-fiction. In the short 100 years between Wright's birth and Grissom's death, transportation had changed radically.

⁕

Brian Byrn has been Curator at the Midwest Museum of American Art in Elkhart for almost three decades. When I first spoke to him about writing a Foreword for this book, he said he'd had transportation on his mind lately because he was planning an exhibit of "Trains, Planes, and Automobiles" from the Museum's permanent collection. Wow, I thought, that's serendipitous. Then, when Lynn started laying out these pages, she said she had a photograph in mind for page 1, but couldn't recall where it was taken. When she described it to me, I said I knew exactly where it was taken—in Elkhart, where Brian is located. Serendipity, indeed. His Foreword is a perfect overture for *Journey's End,* and I'd like to thank him for his thoughtful contribution.

Lynn and I plan to continue seeking out, and sharing, our state's hidden heritage through our photography books. We feel very fortunate to be able to do what we do together. It continues to be a most enjoyable journey...

"It is good to have an end to journey toward, but it is the journey that matters in the end."
Ursula K. Le Guin, 1929–